I0797649

SPACE SYSTEMS:
PATTERNS AND CYCLES

STARS

Candice Letkeman

LIGHTBOX
openlightbox.com

Go to **www.openlightbox.com** and enter this book's unique code.

ACCESS CODE

LBXP2565

Lightbox is an all-inclusive digital solution for the teaching and learning of curriculum topics in an original, groundbreaking way. Lightbox is based on National Curriculum Standards.

OPTIMIZED FOR

- ✓ **TABLETS**
- ✓ **WHITEBOARDS**
- ✓ **COMPUTERS**
- ✓ **AND MUCH MORE!**

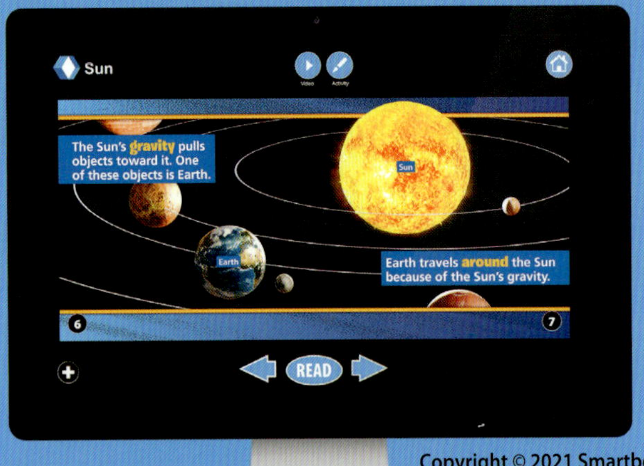

Copyright © 2021 Smartbook Media Inc. All rights reserved.

STANDARD FEATURES OF LIGHTBOX

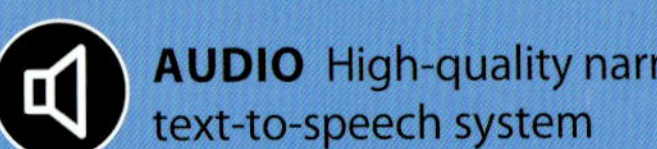
AUDIO High-quality narration using text-to-speech system

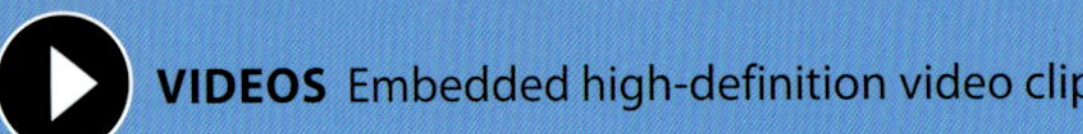
VIDEOS Embedded high-definition video clips

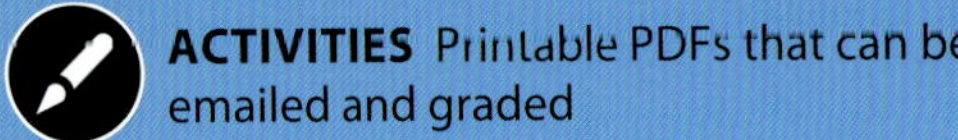
ACTIVITIES Printable PDFs that can be emailed and graded

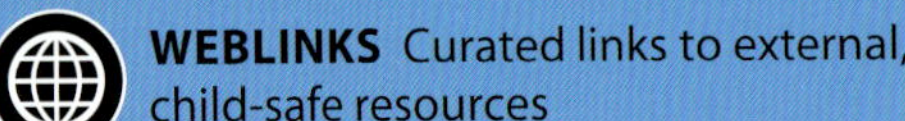
WEBLINKS Curated links to external, child-safe resources

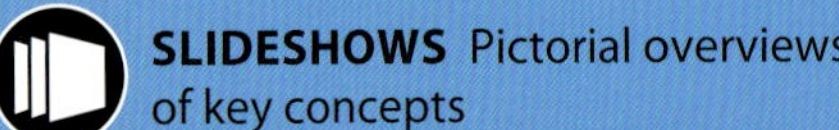
SLIDESHOWS Pictorial overviews of key concepts

INTERACTIVE MAPS Interactive maps and aerial satellite imagery

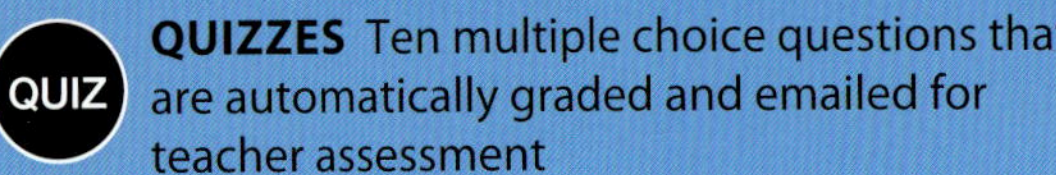
QUIZZES Ten multiple choice questions that are automatically graded and emailed for teacher assessment

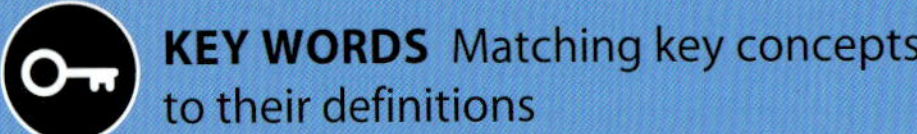
KEY WORDS Matching key concepts to their definitions

VIDEOS

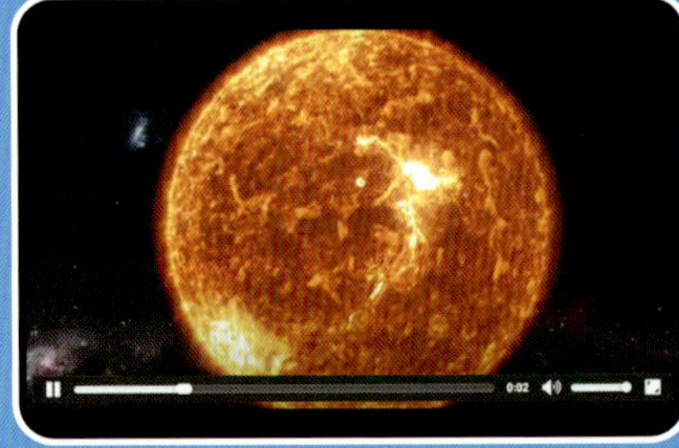

WEBLINKS

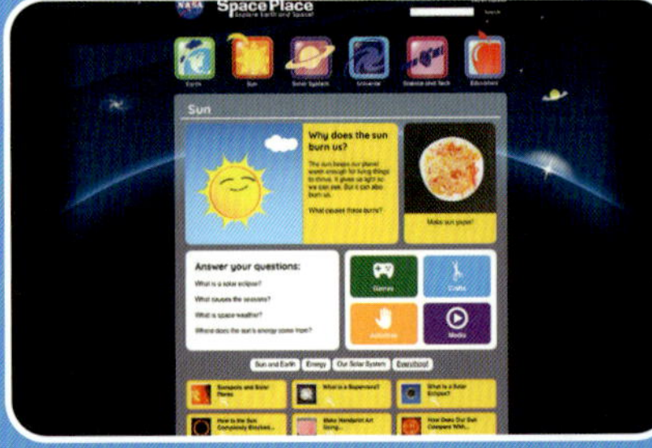

SLIDESHOWS

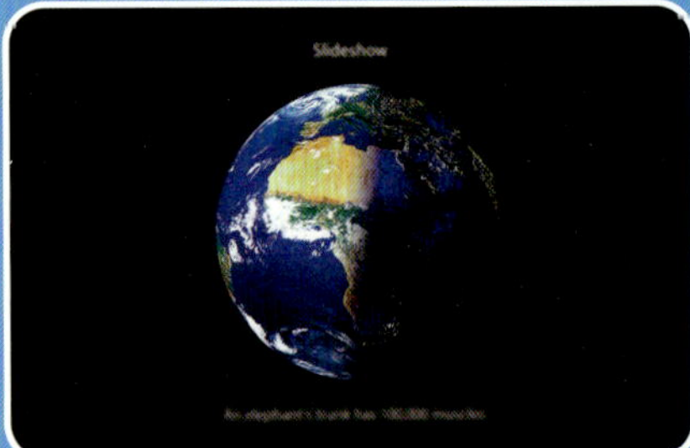

QUIZZES

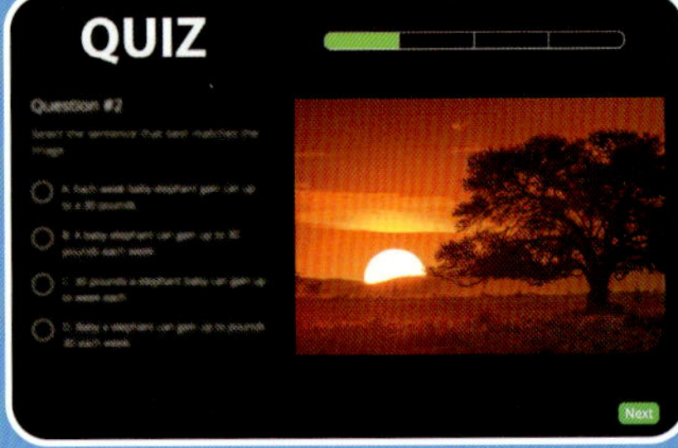

Contents

Stars shine in the **night** sky. People have studied stars for thousands of years.

Stars are huge balls of gas. The **Sun** is a star. It is usually the only star we see in the **day**.

5

There are **billions** of stars in the universe. We only see a few of them.

The **North Star** can only be seen from the northern half of Earth.

Sirius is the **brightest** star in the night sky.

Stars look tiny because they are very **far** away.

Some are so far away that we cannot see them from **Earth**.

People have made maps of the stars. Some stars are in groups called **constellations**.

You can see about **2,000 stars** on a clear night without a telescope.

Constellations can help people **find their way**.

Earth rotates on its **axis**.
This makes the stars appear
to move from **east** to **west**.

Stars are always in the sky, even during the **day**.

The **Sun** shines brighter than other stars, so we only see most stars at **night**.

We can see different stars each **season**.

Some **constellations** are clearer in certain seasons.

We can see **Orion** best in **winter**. It has three stars in a row that make it easy to find.

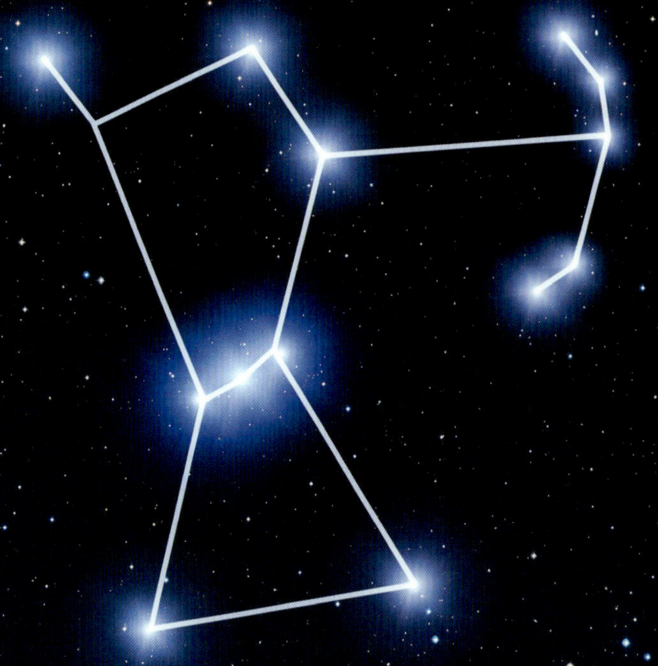

Leo is easy to see in **spring**. Some of its stars make a backward question mark shape.

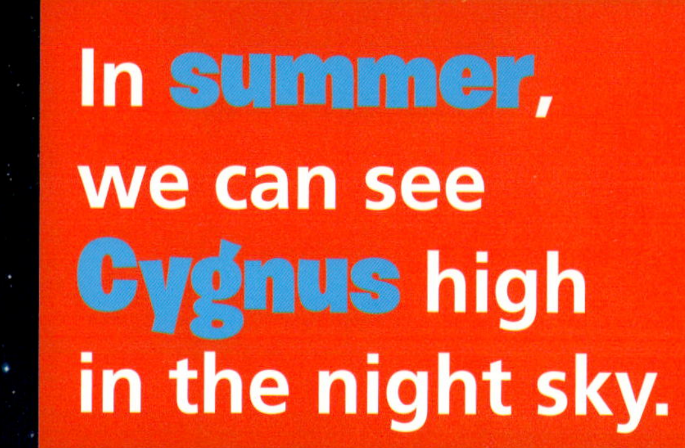

In **summer**, we can see **Cygnus** high in the night sky.

Fall is the best time to see **Cassiopeia**. It has a "W" shape.

Scientists study stars using **telescopes** and cameras.

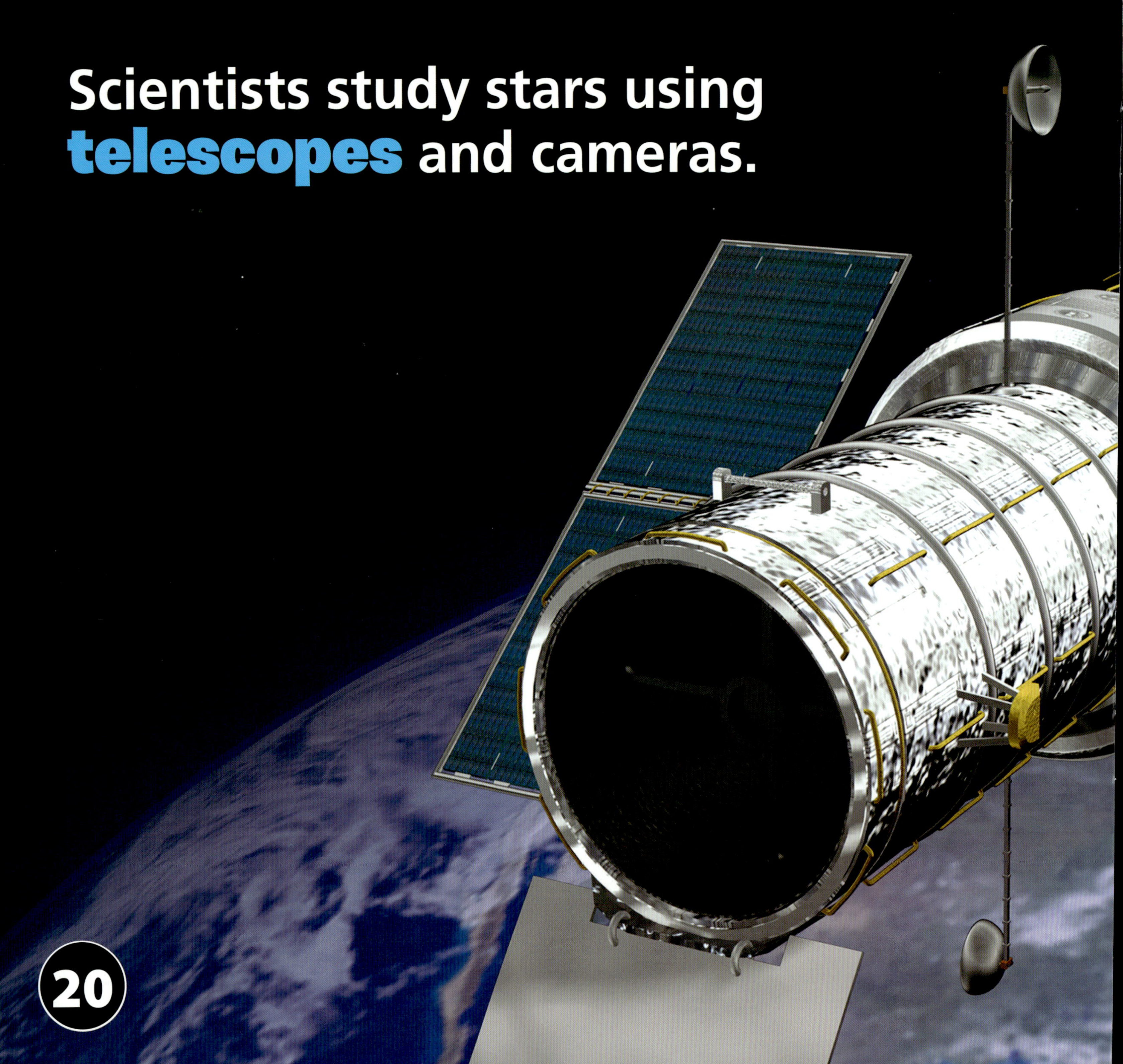

The **Hubble Space Telescope** is a large telescope in space. It takes pictures of stars and sends them to Earth.

The **Hubble Space Telescope** was launched from the **Kennedy Space Center** in **Florida**.

Activity: Day and Night

When can most stars be seen in the sky? Observe the stars in the day and at night. Draw what you see.

Steps

1. You will need a piece of paper and a pencil.
2. Draw a line down the middle of the paper.
3. Write “Day” on one side of the line. Draw the star you see in the day.
4. Write “Night” on the other side of the line. Draw the stars you see at night.

Did you see any stars during the day? What about at night?

KEY WORDS

Research has shown that as much as 65 percent of all written material published in English is made up of 300 words. These 300 words cannot be taught using pictures or learned by sounding them out. They must be recognized by sight. This book contains 65 common sight words to help young readers improve their reading fluency and comprehension. This book also teaches young readers several important content words, such as proper nouns. These words are paired with pictures to aid in learning and improve understanding.

Page	Sight Words First Appearance
4	a, are, day, for, have, in, is, it, night, of, only, people, see, the, we, years
6	few, them, there
7	be, can, Earth, from
8	away, because, far, look, they, very
9	so, some, that
10	about, groups, made, on, without, you
11	find, help, their, way
12	its, makes, move, this, to
14	always, even
15	at, most, other, than
16	different, each
18	has, three
19	high, time
20	and, study
21	large, pictures, takes, was

Page	Content Words First Appearance
4	balls, gases, sky, stars, Sun
6	universe
7	North Star, Sirius
10	constellations, maps, telescope
12	axis, east, west
16	season
18	Leo, Orion, row, shape, spring, winter
19	Cassiopeia, Cygnus, fall, summer
20	cameras, scientists
21	Florida, Hubble Space Telescope, Kennedy Space Center, space

Published by Smartbook Media Inc.
14 Penn Plaza, 9th Floor New York, NY 10122
Website: www.openlightbox.com

Copyright ©2021 Smartbook Media Inc.
All rights reserved. No part of this publication may be reproduced, stored in a retrieval system, or transmitted in any form or by any means, electronic, mechanical, photocopying, recording, or otherwise, without the prior written permission of the publisher.

Library of Congress Control Number: 2020936991

ISBN 978-1-5105-5528-0 (hardcover)
ISBN 978-1-5105-5529-7 (multi-user eBook)

Printed in Guangzhou, China
1 2 3 4 5 6 7 8 9 0 24 23 22 21 20

052020
110819

Project Coordinator: Priyanka Das
Designer: Ana María Vidal

Every reasonable effort has been made to trace ownership and to obtain permission to reprint copyright material. The publisher would be pleased to have any errors or omissions brought to its attention so that they may be corrected in subsequent printings.

The publisher acknowledges Getty Images, iStock, and Shutterstock as the primary image suppliers for this title.